# how to
# piss off
# men

T0182724

## 109 THINGS TO SAY TO SHATTER THE MALE EGO

# how to piss off men

### KYLE PRUE

For my grandpa

## DAVID EDWARD PRUE

*A man so great he ruined the rest of 'em for me.*

Published by Sourcebooks
P.O. Box 4410, Naperville, Illinois 60567–4410
(630) 961-3900
sourcebooks.com

Cataloging-in-Publication Data is on file with the Library of Congress.

Printed and bound in the United States of America.
KP 10 9 8 7 6 5 4 3 2 1

# HOW TO USE THIS BOOK

---

## PISSING SOMEONE OFF IS NOT, STRICTLY SPEAKING, A GOOD OR NICE THING TO DO.

Glad we got that out of the way.

However, if you are going to do it, I recommend doing it discreetly and with surgical precision. Any middle-school girl can tell you that, as far as psychological warfare is concerned, a statement has *nothing* on a question. While a cruel statement can do damage, the bluntness of it often implies malice. And malice implies motivation that comes from somewhere other than the truth.

Take this statement, for instance: "You look like you can't swim." Ouch. That's a cutting thing to say to anyone. But your intent rests right on the surface: *I want to hurt your feelings.* And your intended opponent's brain will eventually entrench itself against its clear enemy: you. Instead of thinking, *I look like I can't swim*, he'll think, *Well, fuck you.*

Now, what if we turn that statement into a question, asked with earnestness: "Can you swim?" A question implies interest and concern. Furthermore, it masks your true intent: dissection.

He'll internalize this question. And whether the answer is yes or no, he will eventually get to our cruel statement all on his own: *I look like I can't swim.* The greatest weapon of the emotional assassin is their target's own synapses.

If he's gone to therapy, this likely won't work (which means it's very likely to work).

Now, you might be asking, "Kyle, isn't this a form of gaslighting?"

No. You sound crazy.

You gotta stop talking to those "friends" of yours.

# DISCLAIMER

—

## SELF-AWARENESS IS A DYING ART FORM. THIS IS MY BEST SWING AT IT.

I am a cis white man. While I think that's been very useful in researching this book and explaining the male psyche, there are things that I can feel comfortable saying and doing that other groups (women, BIPOC, trans individuals, etc.) can't.

Please only use the insults in this book if you feel safe and comfortable doing so. Public spaces and witnesses are not only good armor; they're a good audience too.

## *"NO."*

---

This one's a classic. Total banger. It's been putting numbers on the board since the formation of Indo-European languages.

# "YOU'RE LIKE THE MALE AMY SCHUMER."

—

I'm not sure what exactly Amy Schumer did to elicit such omnipresent rage, but the male psyche appears to be allergic to the very mention of her. I've found this one to be nearly one hundred percent successful.

When he asks why you said this, say, "Oh, it's just, like...I don't know. Something about your energy reminds me of her."

# "ARE YOU IN THE JROTC?"

—

Say this to someone in the real military.

**WARNING:**

Make sure you do it on American soil.

# "OH, SO IT'S LIKE KOHL'S CASH?"

—

Say this when a man tries to explain crypto to you.

# "OH! I SAW THAT ON PINTEREST!"

—

Say this when a man talks about anything he's interested in or shows you one of his tattoos. This is a great way to do two things:

1. Drive a stake into the heart of his ambitions of originality.
2. Get the words of the iconic stand-up comedian Ali Wong ringing in his head: "If a man has a Pinterest, he's probably Pinterest-ed in men."

# "YOU'RE SO FRUGAL."

—

This is a good trick to get a man to spend more money on you. The next time he's in line at Trader Joe's and sees the bouquets of flowers, he'll think, *Oh, I'll show you frugal.*

# "MAYBE YOU'LL FEEL DIFFERENTLY ABOUT THAT WHEN YOU'RE OLDER."

———

Some of the best things to piss off men are really just verbal reverse cards like in Uno. This line has always been a favorite among smug professors and conservative uncles trying to stamp out any mindset that seems borderline "progressive." To pull it on them before they can pull it on you is the metaphysical equivalent of a sucker punch.

**DOUBLE DAMAGE:**

Use this on a Libertarian.

# "I LOVE YOUR COSPLAY."

—

Say this to a man wearing a jersey. When he says, "It's not cosplay," respond by saying, "Well it kind of is… You're not really a basketball player."

# "I WAS THINKING ABOUT YOUR POSTURE THE OTHER DAY..."

—

My roommate used this on me once, and I had to immediately turn my head away so she couldn't see the tears forming in my eyes.

**BONUS POINTS:**
Make it sound like the prelude to an intervention.

# "OH! THEY SANG THIS ON GLEE!"

—

Say this when a man is playing you a classic rock song. This does not have to be true. Odds are he won't know. And if he does know, I'm almost certain he won't tell you.

# "IN THE NEXT BATMAN MOVIE, THE JOKER SHOULD BE A WOMAN."

—

When he presses you on this, say, "Well, women are more persecuted in society, so I think she'd have actual things to be upset about." As he stares at you in stunned silence, finish him off with, "And maybe Tom Holland can play Batman!"

**CAUTION:**

Saying this to the wrong man will turn him into the Joker in real life.

# "YOU SEEM TO BE HAVING A LOT OF FEELINGS RIGHT NOW."

—

If this is not true when you say it, it will be by the time you're finished speaking.

# "OH TRUST ME, WE'VE TALKED ABOUT IT."

—

Men hate being discussed, because it's how they get caught.

# "YOU REMIND ME OF JAMES CORDEN."

---

When he asks why you've said such a thing, respond with, "Oh, you're just funny in the way that he's funny."

Even men who like James Corden don't want to be James Corden.

# "OH MY GOD, YOU'RE SO FUNNY."

———

It is imperative that you deadpan this one. At the very most, you can give him a perplexed half smile. If you overdo this, he will start doing stand-up, and it will be your fault.

# "WHY DON'T WE JUST PRINT MORE MONEY?"

—

Odds are if you say this, he'll respond by smugly saying, "Because of inflation."

That's when you give him a confused look and go, "Oh, honey, no. What you're afraid of is called *hyperinflation*. Leading capitalist economists actually encourage inflation at a rate of about two or three percent per year to stimulate a need for investment and prevent deflation. Deflation is... Well, you know, I really don't feel like explaining deflation right now."

Any pool shark can tell you that this move is called a hustle. However, using it in this context is called the "Finance Bro Honeypot."

# "I LOVE YOUR PRIDE SHIRT."

—

Say this to a man who is wearing a Pink Floyd *Dark Side of the Moon* shirt.

# "I LOVE YOUR SPANX!"

—

Say this to a man who is wearing compression shorts. He's going to try to tell you that they're different from Spanx. He will be wrong.

# "OH, SO IT'S KIND OF LIKE THE BACHELOR?"

—

Say this to a man who is trying to explain the NFL draft.

# "YOU'RE KIND OF LIKE ICARLY!"

—

Say this to a Twitch streamer. (He should be so lucky.)

# "OH MY GOD, I LOVE ANIME! HAVE YOU SEEN RICK AND MORTY?"

—

If you do this one well enough, he'll mutter something in Japanese and run away with his arms behind his back.

**WARNING:**

Do not do this if he is in possession of the Death Note.

# "IS THIS CHRISTIAN ROCK?"

—

Say this when he plays music for you in the car.

**DOUBLE DAMAGE:**

Say this about his unreleased EP.

# "HOW DID ANAKIN GET REY'S LIGHTSABER?"

———

Say this to a Star Wars fan.

**WARNING:**

If you say this loudly enough at a Comic Con, you will most certainly be killed in the worst-smelling riot in history.

# "OH MY GOD, YOU'RE SUCH A BOYBOSS."

—

He's going to ask what this is, to which you'll reply, "It's like a girlboss but a boy."

# "SORRY, I DON'T HAVE ANY CHANGE."

—

Say this to a man who is catcalling you.

**WARNING:**

Please reread the disclaimer at the front of this book.

# "YOU LOOK LIKE YOU'D BE A SLOW RUNNER."

—

Say this to a man when you want him to leave at his greatest possible speed.

**WARNING:**

He *will* realize you're being an asshole, but by the time he does, he'll be half a mile away.

# "IS THE BIG SPOON THE WINNER?"

—

Say this to a man who is watching MMA.

## "I COULD NEVER PICTURE YOU CAMPING."

—

Say this to a man who you're tired of having around the house.

# CALL HIS OUTBURST A HISSY FIT.

—

**WARNING:**

Don't do this if he's passed the threshold of wall punching.

**NOTE:**

Why do men punch walls anyway?

Well, surprisingly enough, there is a strange historical logic to it. From Sun Tzu to the walls of Troy, man's most consistent challenge has been anything that keeps him out.

Men love to imply that violence is somehow

"important," like it draws some comparison between themselves and those Greek warriors of old. But in reality, it's sort of just a fussy thing to do. As he pulls his arm back, dressed in drywall, he probably thinks he resembles some Homeric hero, blithely unaware of the fact that he more closely resembles a toddler in a grocery store.

# "WHAT'S YOUR RELATIONSHIP WITH YOUR MOTHER LIKE?"

---

Say this in response to something blatantly misogynistic. The goal of this is to inspire a sort of dissonance in him. Can he hold his problematic worldview up to a mirror being held by the woman who birthed him? If so... yikes.

# "YOU WOULD BE SUCH A GOOD FRODO."

—

Say this to a man you're watching *Lord of the Rings* with. Then pause and add, "Or actually, you know who you could be?"

He's going to hope for Aragorn.

"Samwise," you'll say.

**NOTE**:

The effectiveness of this depends on how big of a *Lord of the Rings* fan the target is. A true fan will know that Samwise is, in fact, the best character. In this instance, the most devastating burn will be Boromir.

# "WERE YOU HOMESCHOOLED?"

---

This one is verbal buckshot. It's indiscriminate and can clear a room with serious efficiency. However, it has been proven instantly fatal against two kinds of men:

1. Men who went to fancy boarding schools.
2. Men who were homeschooled.

## "HAVE YOU EVER LEFT THE STATE?"

—

Say this to a man who has "I'm better than you because my parents pay for me to go to Europe twice a year" energy.

# "YOU REMIND ME OF ANDY FROM THE OFFICE."

—

Andy is a dark reflection of what any man could become if given enough family money and access to perfect pitch.

In addition, being a strong contender for the least fuckable person at a paper company in Pennsylvania is a herculean failure of charisma. (Ed Helms please don't read this. You're a good actor. Maybe too good.)

# "IS THIS YOUR FIRST TIME ON A PLANE?"

—

**DISCLAIMER:**

This one works best if you're on a plane.

# "I'LL JUST GOOGLE IT."

36

—

Letting a man explain something to you is not unlike letting him have sex with you. I'd even argue that it's a toss-up which activity they enjoy more. In either case, they're building towards some ultimate conclusion (an *oh* and an *O*, respectively). So if you let him explain something for thirty minutes and then say, "I'll just google it," right before he finishes, you can give him the existential equivalent of blue balls.

# "IS THAT A NIFTY?"

—

Say this in reference to an NFT. Bonus points if you can convince him that it's basically a Neopet that launders money.

**DISCLAIMER:**
Much like an NFT, this one will become less valuable as the years go by.

# "WELL, HE IS THE REFEREE. HE'S QUALIFIED TO MAKE THAT CALL."

—

Is this kicking a man while he's down? No. It's arguably curb stomping a man while he's down. Which is worse. Or better. Depends who's doing the kicking.

# "DO YOU HAVE A FRIEND WHO KNOWS A GOOD GYM?"

—

Say this to the most vascular looking man you can find.

# "BEAM ME UP, JOHNNY."

—

Say this when he tells you he's a Star Wars fan.

# "DID YOU KNOW THAT EARLY MEN WERE ACCESSORIES FOR WOMEN? THEY WERE USED TO DEFEND TERRITORY AND FOR PROCREATION."

---

He's going to argue of course. When he does, listen, nod, pause, and ask, "Were you there?"

Now is any of this true? Dunno. Will it make a self-described alpha man's head explode? What won't?

# "DO YOU THINK YOU COULD BEAT A GOOSE IN A FIGHT?"

—

He will, of course, say yes. He'll bring up weight classes, state his resume, etc. The trick here is that no matter what he says, cock your head, consider him carefully, and then say, "But it's a goose..."

**A PERSONAL ANECDOTE:**
This one was used on me once, to devastating effect. I was left feeling adrift. Had I based my entire concept of self-worth on my capacity

for goose violence? I texted a friend for reassurance. Here's how that conversation went:

**KYLE**: Are you reasonably confident in my ability to win a fight to the death with a twenty-pound goose?

**MAX**: What kind of goose are we talking here? Canada, graylag, brant, greater white-fronted?

**KYLE**: Take your strongest pick.

**MAX**: So Canada.

**KYLE**: Geese max out at twenty pounds though. And remember that, though you know me as an improv guy, I was a prizefighter with a nearly perfect record. Although I'm not sure if Muay Thai translates to goose brawling.

**MAX**: Okay, so the giant Canada goose weighs in at 5 kg, or almost 12 lbs.

**KYLE**: I weigh 172 pounds if that matters.

**MAX:** I think you have the edge here, make no mistake—you're a rangy fighter and should have the reach necessary to dispatch the goose with a well-placed kick. Geese are reluctant fighters actually. Their primary defensive response is to try and have a dick-measuring contest with their attacker; male geese will stare down a charging elephant, and usually this is enough to convince an attacker that they're not worth the trouble. What this means is you'd likely have a gimme-strike right at the start, so if you can take him out in one blow, this thing is over before it starts.

**MAX:** My concern is that if it's not enough to take the goose out, you will have one HUGE, seriously pissed-off goose on your hands. I think if it gets you on the ground, it's over—it can just swarm your upper body and overwhelm you. I mean, you're looking at like a seven- or eight-foot wingspan.

**KYLE:** Bro, I am crying reading this.

**KYLE:** This is a fight to the death by the way. No running. If that changes anything.

**MAX:** I would probably bet on you then. 'Cause the goose's only move is to peck your eyes out which like…if the goose is in a position to do that, then you've already lost.

Now what does this prove aside from the fact that there are examples of positive male friendships in the world?

It proves that:

1. This tactic works.
2. I would totally beat a goose in a fight.

## "I LOVE YOUR MOPED."

—

Say this to a man with a Harley.

# "ISN'T THAT THE CAR FROM BACK TO THE FUTURE?"

—

Say this to a man who's talking about *The Mandalorian*.

# "YOU HAVE THE CONFIDENCE OF A MUCH TALLER MAN."

—

Do not use this on a man who you plan to keep a relationship with. There's no coming back from this one.

**NOTE:**
A true short king will take this as a compliment. He built his confidence from the ground up, and it stands taller than he does.

# "YOU'RE SO SASSY."

—

Use this when you feel inclined to call him a dick. Men have spent the last couple thousand years advocating for the importance of dicks and dick-related behavior. All he'll hear is that he's being masculine, firm, and important.

If you elect instead to call him sassy, he'll start to wonder if he moves his arms too much when he talks.

# "I'M HERE."

—

Text him this in the middle of the night and then turn your phone off. Wait as many days as you want and then text him again saying, *Sorry, wrong person.*

## "YOU DANCE JUST LIKE ELLEN!"

—

Say this to a man who you want to start the town from *Footloose*.

# "I LOVE YOUR HAIR. IS IT REAL?"

—

**49**

I will admit, this is not one of mine. I first read this in Neil Strauss's *The Game* (a self-help book about how to insult women into having sex with you).

Do I have a good excuse for having read this book? Well, I was ten at the time (and didn't know what sex was), but even then I should have known that I was far above it (the book, I mean).

Neil Strauss in recent years has come out and declared that *The Game* is pretty much all bullshit (I'm paraphrasing). Maybe because people do change and grow, or maybe because he realized that his manifesto about bedding women was the very thing preventing him from doing so. (There's a valuable lesson here if you're a man who has a podcast about dating.)

Either way, this little insult is the only thing that stuck, and I've found that it's twice as effective against men as it is against women. Funny how that works.

# "ARE YOU CIRCUMCISED?"

—

**50**

Say this to a man who you've had sex with. This will set him on a never-ending mental quest. Was his performance forgettable? Or merely his member? (I apologize for using the word *member*. I wanted the alliteration.)

# "FANTASY FOOTBALL IS JUST DUNGEONS AND DRAGONS FOR PEOPLE WHO ARE BAD AT BOTH FANTASY AND FOOTBALL."

—

Is this a little wordy? Yes. Is it true? Also yes.

# "WOW, THESE NEW TOYOTAS LOOK AWESOME!"

—

Say this to a man who drives a Tesla.

**DOUBLE DAMAGE:**

Stand next to a shitty car that's the same color as his and say, "Babe, unlock it."

# "ARE YOU GUYS WATCHING MEN'S BASKETBALL?"

———

In fact, start calling all sports "men's" sports. Baseball, football, hockey, boxing, whatever.

You might now feel inclined to say, "Hey, Kyle. I'm tracking a theme here. Are the majority of the things you can say to piss off men just repurposed language that men use to discuss women's behavior and activities?"

To which I would probably say, "Oh dang! Yeah, I guess so."

In response to that, I assume you'd say, "Why do you think that is?"

I'd then say something kind of dry but telling, like, "Well, I'm no psychologist, but..."

And then we'd give each other knowing looks.

# "DOESN'T THAT MEAN, 'I'M GONNA FUCK JOE BIDEN'?"

———

Say this to a man who's said, "Let's go, Brandon."

He will respond by saying, "No, it means, 'Fuck Joe Biden.'"

To which you will respond, "I'm not hearing a difference."

(Is this particular entry going to age well? Probably not. Ideally none of it will.)

# "I LOVE DAD BODS! LIKE JASON MOMOA!"

—

**55**

Does this one contribute to the very real issue of unrealistic body standards? I don't know. Maybe. One thing at a time, guys. I'm not a miracle worker; I'm a collection of thirty rats operating a person suit via tiny levers and pulleys. (This statement is, of course, also an unrealistic body standard. In the sense that it's not real and I'm lying.)

# "ISN'T THAT GRIMES'S EX-BOYFRIEND?"

—

Say this to an Elon Musk stan.

# "THIS REMINDS ME OF A DRAG SHOW I WENT TO ONCE."

—

**57**

Say this to a man who's watching WWE.

# "SO YOU'RE, LIKE, A DISNEY ADULT?"

—

Say this to a man who likes Star Wars or Marvel. Some of these hurt because they're factual.

58

# "HAVE YOU EVER HEARD OF ROGAINE?"

—

**59**

This one pairs well with a glass of red and a small but unmistakable glance towards his hairline.

# "THIS REMINDS ME OF HAMILTON."

—

Say this when he plays rap in the car. The better his taste, the worse this one stings.

**60**

# "I'M ONLY A SOCIALIST BECAUSE JESUS WAS."

—

Say this to a man who thinks Jesus was white.

## "I'VE PICKED UP A MINOR IN GENDER POETRY."

—

Say this to kill your grandpa. It's like an octogenarian "off" button.

# "TEAM JACOB, EH?"

—

Say this to a man with a wolf tattoo.

## "I'M A GAMER TOO!"

—

When he asks what game you play, tell him that you're nationally ranked in Webkinz. He'll either have to accept the ridiculous thing you've just said or admit that he knows the ins and outs of the Webkinz interface.

# "THAT LOOKS A LITTLE RARE FOR YOU."

—

Say this when his steak arrives.

**65**

**BONUS POINTS:**
Do it in front of the waiter.

# "OH, LIKE HANNAH MONTANA."

—

Say this to a man who is trying to explain to you the concept of a secret identity.

## "CAN YOU RIDE A BIKE?"

—

The more quiet skepticism you can show in response to his answer, the better.

## "I'LL JUST TEXT MY DAD AND ASK HIM HOW TO DO IT."

———

Hanging up shelves, frying an egg, raking leaves—whatever it is, assume he has *no idea* what he's doing.

**OPTIONAL:**

This one has a nice little sociological benefit. The more you do it, the more you can unwittingly pit him against patriarchal structures. "No, babe, I can do this. The only reason you think your dad knows everything is because society has built structures that have forced you to show him undue reverence."

# "AW, SHE'S SO CUTE. IS SHE A DOODLE?"

—

Say this about a man's rottweiler, German shepherd, pit bull, or feral child.

# "I'M FIVE FOOT TEN."

—

Say this to a man when you are actually six foot one.

This one is, of course, only useful to my male readership (if you are out there) and my tall queens.

I've been doing this for years, and it never fails to break a feeble spirit. I've even had my license changed and designed a tape measure with three missing inches. Do I have too much time on my hands? We wouldn't be here if I didn't.

# "DO YOU WANT THAT VEGETARIAN OR NOT VEGETARIAN?"

—

Say this to a man who is ordering food from you.

71

# "HAVE YOU EVER SEEN CAILLOU?"

—

Say this to a man who is talking about Andrew Tate since he loves listening to bald toddlers so much.

Is *this one* going to age well? Probably not. But neither is Andy.

# "YOU'RE SUCH A JOE ROGAN GUY."

—

This works very well on men who like Joe Rogan and men who hate Joe Rogan.

If he does like Joe Rogan, say, "Oh my god, I've fallen in *love* with his podcast after finding out it's satire."

# "THERE ARE MORE BISEXUAL PEOPLE THAN STRAIGHT PEOPLE NOW."

—

Say this to your local homophobe. Is it true? Maybe!

74

# "YOU'VE BEEN SERVED."

—

When I first moved to Los Angeles, I was unemployed and looking for recreational ways to sow discord. I am what's known as a "high sensation-seeking individual," a person with a proclivity for boredom. Deadly boredom. Unchecked, we sensation-seekers can veer off into crocodile wrangling, drug use, or cult leadership. I'm told that if you want to survive *l'appel du vide,* your best friend is a "healthy" outlet. I thought I'd cracked it for a while, but there's only so many times you can go skydiving before you go broke. Google the price of jet fuel if you don't believe me.

Anyway, that's how I became a process server.

It started with Margot, a friend of a friend, who called me to ask if I'd be comfortable serving her asshole husband his divorce papers. Boy, would I.

The more I learned about my target, Jason, the more I began to see my messenger mission as a kind of vigilantism. I was the Batman of Broken Marriages. A kid on Christmas. I slept cradling my manila folder like a teddy bear.

Margot had warned me that Jason fancied himself a psychic. "What does that even mean?" my roommate asked. "Like the way rats can tell when trains are coming?" I neglected to mention that humans can do that too, because trains run very loud and on schedule. Jason however, didn't do either of those things. He was silent and erratic. A process server's worst nightmare.

He quickly made a believer out of me. Slipping from my grasp time after time, not unlike the unwrangleable crocodiles of my youth.

When I showed up at his job, he called out sick. When I saw him on the street, he ducked into an alley. I spent months stalking this guy, and in a way, I never wanted it to end. He was my nemesis. A prize-winning buck. A snake with infinite skin to shed.

I did eventually catch him. Some Saturday morning, I was listening to an interview from a hunter. "Want to get a rabbit, shoot twice," he said, southernly. "Shoot twice in the same place. They run in circles, so if you miss with the first bullet, he'll run into the second."

I gasped.* That was it.

I drove to Jason's place of employment, a

* For the first and only time in my life.

stall at the Santa Monica Farmer's Market, and asked his coworkers if he was around. They told me he'd called out. As per usual. So I left. As per usual. Except this time, I returned a half hour later and found Jason crouching over a box of artichokes. I placed the folder delicately in front of him, and he glared up at me, looking like a steaming rabbit stew. "You've been served." I told him.

Euphoric antagonism. I think of him often. My one that got away. For a time at least.

Process serving was a brief yet crackling chapter of my life. I abandoned it quickly when I discovered that I didn't need the long arm of the law to piss off men. Turns out I could do it pretty much anywhere, and with less of a paper trail. I suppose this is my origin story. Every vigilante has one.

## "I LIKE YOUR BLOUSE."

—

You can use this one on pretty much any man (provided he's wearing a shirt).

# "DO YOU NEED ME TO WALK YOU TO YOUR CAR?"

—

Say this to a man who suspects he's the only thing standing between you and certain death.

# "WERE YOU ON THE TOPLESS TEAM?"

—

Say this to a man who has just finished a game of shirts vs. skins.

# "DO YOU
WORK HERE?"

—

Say this to a man who is waiting for his wife to
finish up shopping.

## "WERE YOU BORN PREMATURE? YOU KIND OF GIVE ME A PREEMIE VIBE."

—

This was said to me three weeks ago to the day. I am going to be vulnerable with you, reader. It lodged beneath my skin like a steel splinter. In every free moment, I am reminded of the barb, lying insidiously beneath the surface. I fled the country to escape it. But on the shores of the Greek island of Paros, it remains within me. Like some metal mutation.

Not that it matters, but I was born eight pounds, four ounces, and two weeks late because my mother didn't want a Leo. Yes, I am a

Virgo. If you hadn't suspected that on some level, that's on you. Who publishes a list of insults? That's Virgo shit.

In correcting these things in print, I recognize that this book has become a grotesque autobiography of my insecurities. And that's okay. That's literature. And I'm only a man.

I'm going insane. Send help. I'm on the beach in Paros. I'm the one with the preemie vibe.

# "MY FAVORITE RAPPER IS BROCKHAMPTON. HE'S AWESOME."

—

Say this to the biggest hip-hop fan you can find. Don't get it? Don't worry. He will. And that's all that matters.

# "I LOVE YOUR PIXIE CUT."

—

Say this to a man with short hair.

# "DO YOU MEAN BARITENOR?"

———

Say this to a theater boy who tells you he's a tenor. This one is niche, but you can use it to destroy a BFA program within a week.

**BONUS POINTS:**

Use this on Ed Helms. (I told you to stop reading.)

# "ARE THOSE BOWLING SHOES?"

—

Say this when a self-professed "sneakerhead" shows you his latest acquisition.

# "OOH-LA-LA!"

—

Say this when he tells you he attended an ivy league university. Men from America's "best and brightest" institutions ruin any cool factor that it affords them by never shutting the fuck up about it for the rest of their lives. You know what type of guys I'm talking about. The type that would get annoyed at me for "forgetting" to capitalize *ivy league* in my nationally published book.

Here's the full version of this technique:

**VICTIM**: I went to Penn.

**YOU**: Penn State?

**VICTIM**: No, Penn.

**YOU**: What's the difference?

**VICTIM**: Penn is an Ivy.

**YOU**: Ooh-la-la.

# "I LOVE YOUR JEANS! THEY MAKE YOU LOOK SO...EUROPEAN."

———

Say this to a homegrown country boy.

American men hate to be reminded of their natural enemies, the Europeans. I understand. They can be infuriating. With their...purses and...ability to pleasure a woman.

# "WOULD SHE LIKE
# A KID'S MENU?"

---

Say this to a man on a date with a much younger woman.

This one is dangerous. Indiscriminate shrapnel everywhere. Only employ it if you don't mind his date getting caught in the cross fire.

# "YOU MIGHT WANT TO TAKE A FEW TRIPS."

—

Say this to a man when you want him to crush himself under the weight of a dozen Costco boxes. Buy in bulk, die in bulk.

## "I'M SURE SHE'LL BE REALLY SAD WHEN YOU DIE ALONE."

———

Say this to a man who is complaining about being "friend-zoned."

I actually got this one from an AI that my friend Lucas Simon coded to write some things you can say to piss off men (we called it "the Misandroid").

Unfortunately, a being that runs on logic had little luck understanding or unraveling the male ego. I guess that means my job is safe (for now).

At least, before our robot went insane and poured a cup of coffee on itself,* it was able to spit out this total banger.

<hr />

* After we told it I majored in gender poetry.

## "THIS SONG REMINDS ME OF YOU."

—

Text him this and then send him any Meghan Trainor song (excluding "Dear Future Husband").

If he inquires why, tell him that it's something about his general aura. This will damn him to an eternal vicious cycle of failure and frustration: *How can I purge this Meghan Trainor-esque quality from myself without taking the time to learn what an aura is?*

# "DON'T EAT THAT NEAR HIM! HE'S ALLERGIC TO PEANUTS."

—

Say this about him to someone else. He'll say, "Wait, I'm not allergic to peanuts."

Take a *long pause*... Look bewildered. Finally say, "Huh. Why did I think that?"

# "OH MY GOD, I HAD NO IDEA! I JUST WANT YOU TO KNOW THAT I'M AN ALLY."

—

Say this reassuringly when he tells you he's a "man's man" or a "guy's guy."

# "OH, IT'S LIKE TAROT!"

—

Say this to a man who is talking about Magic:
The Gathering. Or Yu-Gi-Oh! Or poker.

## "I FEEL LIKE YOU'D REALLY THRIVE IN MUSICAL THEATER."

—

Say this to someone who would *not*.

# "DO YOU HAVE A HUMILIATION FETISH?"

—

Say this to a man who thinks he's impressing you.

## "I THOUGHT YOUR VOICE WOULD BE DEEPER."

—

Say this if you feel like torpedoing a Hinge date.

## "THAT TRACKS."

—

Say this when he tells you his star sign.

## "YOU GIVE ME RA VIBES."

—

Let him know he's the type to dance at orientation.

**NOTE:**
In case you were wondering, ACAB includes RAs.

# "WERE YOU A LEASH KID?"

—

Say this to a man who you want to sit still.

**WARNING:**

Do not say this to a man who you suspect even a little bit to be a furry. This will activate him like a Russian sleeper agent.

# "ARE YOU ON ANTIBIOTICS?"

—

Say this apropos of nothing. To you, he's not a sexual prospect. He's a petri dish.

# "HUH. THAT'S SO INTERESTING. YOU SOUND REALLY SMART."

—

This one requires a *lot* of emphasis on the word *sound.*

# "DID YOU MAKE THAT UP?"

—

Say this when a self-described "comedian" says something "clever." This one has a nice compounding effect. The first time you do it, he'll smugly say, "Well, yes. I did." But by the fourth or fifth time, he'll realize that you doubt his capacity for independent thought.

# "HAVE YOU CONSIDERED GROWING A BEARD?"

—

Say this to a man with a beard.

# "DAMN, SHE SOUNDS COOL."

—

Say this when a man is complaining about something his "crazy ex" did to him.

Alternatively, you could say, "Whoa... Legend."

# "I LOVE YOUR CORSET."

—

Say this to man who is wearing a weight belt.

# "AT A MALL?"

—

Say this when he tells you he's a cop.

**WARNING:**

Make sure his body cam is on.

# "IS THAT A FURRY THING?"

—

Say this when he tells you he's an "alpha male." If all else fails, bark at him until he realizes he's not really about that life.

# "YOU SMELL A LOT BETTER THAN I THOUGHT YOU WOULD."

—

This one will make him happy for a few seconds and then sad for the rest of his life.

## "I LIKE YOUR BRACELET."

—

Say this to a man who is wearing a Rolex.

# A GUIDE TO CREATING YOUR OWN INSULT

—

When my Things to Say to Piss Off Men series originally went viral on the internet, a certain contingent of people (guess their demographic) decided to threaten my mother.

Naturally, this sent me into an immediate panic. But not for the reason you might expect. Kelly Prue once sewed her own face back together after a motorcycle crash in France because she didn't trust a student nurse to do it. Upon returning to America, her plastic surgeon frowned at her and said, "These stitches are kind of crooked."

"Well, I did them myself," my mother said, without a hint of personal pride.

If she were so willing to dig through her own flesh in the corner room of a French student hospital, I couldn't imagine what she'd do to anyone trying to threaten her in her own home. I'm sure these "trolls," or whatever we're calling them now, were aware that they might be poking a bear. However, they were, in fact, poking a bomb.

My mother's advice has always been, as you might assume, direct. She's a nice person but not an overly pleasant person. (I mean that literally, in that she does not care for pleasantries.) She told me once, "Women want to feel loved, and men want to feel important." At the time, I said, "Mom, you're generalizing."

I'm not qualified to speak to the first one, but as to the second, it's become the primary foundation of my technique. Men want to feel important. I'd venture to say that many—if not all—of the darkest chapters in history can be attributed to the male quest for importance. Why start a war? Because war is important (and penetrative). What a way to blow off steam. What a way to self-actualize.

Therefore, to truly piss off a man and make your own insult, all you need to do is locate the structure that he derives importance from, and then belittle it. His sad little brain will do the fatal calculus all by itself.

# WHY TO PISS OFF MEN

—

Why do I care if I can beat a goose in a fight? Or more accurately (since I definitely can), why do I care if I am *perceived* as someone who *could* beat a goose in a fight? I live in Los Angeles. The scenario is unlikely. Why have I (a "reformed" man) built any measure of my identity around my capacity for man-on-goose violence?

If you've read this far, you know that men think anger is an important, direct emotion. In reality, anger is a complicated, amorphous, fluid feeling that seeks to warn us of deeper, scarier, weepier emotions. Anger never shows up first. It follows on the heels of fear, hurt, or loss. Anger is blood from a wound. Men love to talk about the blood and never the wound.

Are you enriching someone's life by pissing them off? Probably not. Definitely not, if they're not willing to treat anger as a messenger, to follow it to its source. But in rare instances, I've seen men grab anger by the hand and follow it with genuine curiosity.

Take my situation, for instance:

The patriarchy depends on structures to sustain itself. In order for it to exist, men need to form their ideals of masculinity around certain qualifiers. You are a man if you _____. In my case, you are a man if you are capable of goose abuse.

The patriarchy is constructed this way so that men feel the need to rush to defend those structures when those structures are threatened. They think that if they *don't*, they will lose the things that make them men. It's that fear of losing their privilege that inspires the anger. Only in following the anger can we interrogate the structure.

Somehow my perception of masculinity had become inextricably tied to one's ability to defend oneself and, if needed, hurt other people.[*] Why is that? Perhaps because I come from a family of fighters. Black belts litter my father's side of the family tree, and it stretches upwards towards my grandfather, a black belt–having, tattoo-wearing, motorcycle-riding badass. Did I form these associations on purpose? No. I just love and admire the men of my family very much, and somewhere along the way I had decided that in order to be admirable like them, I had to be capable of fighting like them.

When I think about my grandfather though, it's not the fighting that I remember. One memory sticks out:

............

[*] Or geese.

In recent years my grandfather has lost the majority of his memory and motor skills to dementia. When I go to visit him, I always make sure to bring a slice of Starbucks lemon cake (his favorite treat). And every time, without fail, he splits the cake into pieces so he can share it with me (a total stranger).

To me, this is the most selfless act I have ever witnessed. It floors me to see a man remember to be kind, even when he's forgotten everything else. To me, this stands head and shoulders above the infinite feats of his life. To me this is the trait most worth embodying.

And to think, this realization only came to me when I was willing to follow my anger. To circumnavigate the hulking metaphorical goose that had overwhelmed my sleepless nights, to reconnect to someone who I felt like I had lost.

Did I write this book so that women could learn to bully men? No. Did I write this book because I hate men? No. (This section also functions as my FAQ.) I wrote this book because I think it's time for men to take our cultural medicine. To let our anger inform us of our hurt and finally heal from it.

If you happen to be a man, and you happen to have read this far, I'd like to leave you with a final visual metaphor.

The patriarchy puts women in a box. And then it puts men in their own box on top of that one. And on some level, men think that qualifies as a win. But at the end of the day, everyone's still trapped in a box. We men are all trapped in there together. With our anger, our egos, and maybe a goose or two.

# ACKNOWLEDGMENTS

—

If you're glad this book exists, you owe your thanks to my book agent Jon Michael Darga who caught me in the wild, duct taped me to a chair, and convinced me that this was something the world needed. To think we almost missed out on all this fun (and $$$). Additional thanks to some of Jon's colleagues at Aevitas Creative Management, Kate Mack, Mags Chmielarczyk, Dierdre Smerillo, and Melissa Moorehead who handled my contracts, and Maggie Cooper and Lily Stephens from the payment team.

I'd also like to offer my highest thanks to Kate Roddy, my editor at Sourcebooks who steered *How To Piss Off Men* to its rightful home and sharpened it to a deadly point. It's warmed what's left of my heart to see my jokes protected and prepared for the big time with such care.

Speaking of HTPOM's rightful home, I'd love to thank my incredible Sourcebooks marketing team, primarily Madeleine Brown and Kayleigh George, who have fielded my manic emails and empowered my stranger strategies. The fact that this book is in your hands is testament to their talent.

Other helping hands at Sourcebooks include Emily Proano, my production editor, and Brittany Vibbert, my art director. A huge thanks to them for making sure this thing came out complete.

I'd also like to thank anyone who makes an appearance in this book, whether named on the page or not. Jasmine Melody, Max Michalsky, Lucas Simon, Jill Garner, Rachael Slakter, Zoe Duncan-Doroff, Margot, Margot's scumbag ex-husband, Kelly Prue, and of course David Edward Prue.

Though he goes unmentioned within its pages, this book is overflowing with my father's signature style of self-deprecating wit. He taught me from the moment I became sentient that as a comedian you belong within your joke, and not above it or outside it. I'd be remiss not to include an incredibly special shoutout to my writing partner, and most frequent collaborator Joseph Johnston. I've sharpened my words and wit against his for nearly a decade now, and somehow, enthrallingly, it feels like we're only just beginning.

And finally, I'd like to thank everyone who's ever pitched me a "thing you can say to piss off men." Whether over drinks, shouted at me through my open car window, or left in my comment section, I've been inspired by a litany of antagonists from all over the world. It's been my honor to assemble this almanac for you, and to make this world a little more sour.

# ABOUT THE AUTHOR

—

Kyle Prue is a famous author and gender traitor. He was untimely ripped from his mother during the Detroit blackout at the ripe age of zero. As a child he was expelled from two elementary schools and the Catholic Church. As a teenager, he attended a philosophy-oriented high school, where he built a shrine to Thomas Hobbes in the woods. He attended college at the University of Michigan, where he studied narcissism and love bombing (acting and poetry). He lives in Los Angeles with three roommates and a tapeworm (all parasites).